I WAS TOLD THAT HE WOULDN'T SURVIVE

MY DEAR SON

JODI LENAGHEN DALY

LifeRich Publishing is a registered trademark of
The Reader's Digest Association, Inc.

LifeRich Publishing books may be ordered through booksellers or by contacting:

LifeRich Publishing
1663 Liberty Drive
Bloomington, IN 47403
www.liferichpublishing.com
1 (888) 238-8637

ISBN: 978-1-4897-2216-4 (sc)
ISBN: 978-1-4897-2215-7 (hc)
ISBN: 978-1-4897-2217-1 (e)

Library of Congress Control Number: 2019903263

Print information available on the last page.

LifeRich Publishing rev. date: 04/09/2019

This book is dedicated to my dear son.

A special "Thank You" to the high school students that have assisted me with Web Design and Graphic Design.

CHAPTER ONE

As I lay there in the morning light, a slight cramp in my lower abdomen awoke me. After a few seconds it disappeared, only to return again at any moment. This took place several times, so the second that my doctor's office opened, at seven o'clock, I called and was told to meet the doctor at the hospital.

I was so scared, so nervous! It was only a little over a month and a half since I had lost the first of the twins. They were in different sacks. "This one had to be alright! I couldn't lose this one also! I'm thirty three years old, I've wanted this baby for so many years. Oh please don't let anything happen to this baby!"

While the doctor examined me, he said, "You are in labor. This baby is coming. You can deliver it here and we will send the baby to Albany. You will need to go separately. Or, we can send you right now to Syracuse and you will deliver the baby there.'

"I want to go to Syracuse so I can stay with my baby", I replied. My heart was pounding! My mind was racing!

I asked one of the nurses to please call my sister Lori and tell her. I was there by myself. I kept praying for the strength and the wisdom to do what I needed to do.

So many things were rushing through my mind. "I was only five months along. Would my baby live or die? What kind of problems would this create for my baby? How would I take care of things? How would I prepare for this baby? How would I work to pay the rent and care for my baby's needs at the same time? Why wasn't the cerclage that was sewn into my cervix holding my baby inside of my uterus?

It had only been a little over a month and a half since I miscarried the first baby of the twins. Even though I was told everything looked alright for this baby, the second of the twins, I still needed to be very careful, which I had been trying to do.

The ambulance ride to Syracuse is a blur. Once at the hospital in Syracuse, the doctors immediately attached leads to my abdomen so they could keep track of the baby. I was so scared that I would lose this baby also! The contractions did not stop coming. I continued by myself. I continued to pray for strength and wisdom.

I was told that, " You are way too early for us to be able to save the baby, if born now. We can try to hold off delivery to keep the baby inside of you for as long as possible. There are no guarantees. Be prepared because, it's very likely that the baby will not make it!"

I told the doctor, "I don't care what I have to go through! Please, do what you need to do! I can't lose this baby!"

The days all ran together. I could eat and drink very little. Too many times to count, the nurses came running in to help me because, once again, I was having a full contraction.

I had spent so much time in tears! "I didn't know how to fix this! I didn't know how to stop this! Now I could lose this baby also! No! I can't lose this one! I've waited too long to have a child!" I laid there completely alone, except for the doctors and nurses.

I continually went over in my mind how careful I had been. Before I became pregnant, I only ate health food. As soon as I found out that I was pregnant. I became even more careful about the food that I ate. I needed to stay very healthy in order to have a healthy baby. None of that even matters now. I still could lose this baby!

After nine days of having contractions, laying flat in the hospital bed, the doctors came in and said, "You are dilated over five centimeters. The cerclage is ripping your cervix, we need to go in and take it out now! Your baby will be born soon!"

The doctors went in and removed the cerclage and wheeled me down to another room. My contractions intensified and came closer together. The hospital called my sister Lori and told her it was time. She called the hospital on another line and I was handed a phone, I could only talk for a short second because the labor pains were very intense. They wheeled me into the labor room.

I was so scared, and so alone. The doctor, and about ten nurses, all doing specific duties. The contractions continued. The doctor kept saying, "Not yet! Not yet! Ok now! Push now!" I pushed, and pushed! Out came my baby! All I heard was silence! I heard no cry! The nurses passed my baby from one to another.

My heart was pounding so hard and so fast! Had my baby died? I kept listening, trying to hear 'the cry'! I heard nothing! I just saw everyone working in silence.

I felt so helpless! It felt like my heart was being ripped out of my chest

A few minutes later an isolette was wheeled up next to me. It had in it, my beautiful son. He was alive! Born at five and a half months gestation, fifteen weeks early. He looked so beautiful, so peaceful and calm, weighing only one pound, twelve ounces. I looked at him, trying to take it all in, and trying to hold on to every detail of his little, round, curled up body. They quickly wheeled him away.

I was afraid that I would never see him again. I had such a lost, helpless feeling!

They brought me to a room so I could clean up. My mind was going so fast, but it kept going back to my precious son. I had a son! I was his mother! The chills were running down my spine! I was so anxious and excited! I needed to get back to him! What if something happened to him and I wasn't there! My mind, once again, was spinning in circles!

The nurse wheeled me down to the Neonatal Intensive Care Unit, the NICU. I was told that the next few hours, and days, if he made it that long, were critical. There were so many machines, needles, and tubes attached to my son. His skin was almost transparent. His bones were still very soft.

'only two hours old! His skin is almost transparent'

I could see that he was crying, but no sound came out. His lungs were not fully formed or developed yet so there was no air going through his vocal chords. I leaned down and very softly started to sing one of three songs that I quite often sang to him before he was born.

He immediately calmed down and returned to sleep. I could reach in and touch him, but I could not hold him or move him. I named him Michael James.

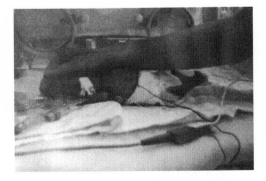

'he was so small!'

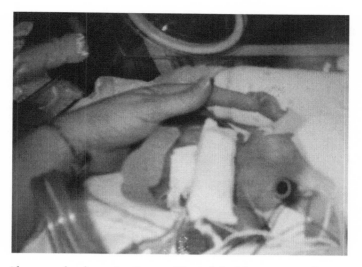

'he reached up by himself and held onto my finger'

The doctors said, " the next couple of days and hours are critical, he may not make it. If he is fortunate enough to make it, he will have many problems, many difficulties. He will be behind in several ways.

He also has WPW, Wolfe Parkinson White. This is an extra electrical pathway in his heart which allows extra electrodes through. Very often his heart rate speeds up, it doubles,which takes a lot of energy and strength out of this little body. We will watch to see how it will effect him in the long run."

I looked at the doctor and very nicely said, "that is my son. He will be fine and he will develop correctly. He will be perfectly fine. After so many years of wanting a child, and now I have a son. There is nothing that can take him from me, nothing!"

I returned to my room. A nurse came in and we talked about the importance of breast milk for the baby. I assured her, "that was already the plan." I was provided with a powerful breast pump, as Michael was not ready to feed on any kind of food yet. I needed to pump it and store it in little bottles in the freezer. She also helped me to make arrangements for accommodations so that I would be able to stay near my son.

My father and sister, Diane, came to visit me for a short time, they had already stopped to see my son, Micheal, and could only see him through the glass. She handed me a little white teddy bear for Michael, seven inches in length.

For the next day and a half I spent every second that I could with my son, pumping every four hours, into little glass bottles. Then the doctor came in and said to me, "you are well enough to be released." I made a phone call and someone came to pick me up.

CHAPTER TWO

I went to my apartment and packed a large suitcase. I drove back out to Syracuse. I checked in to the 'house' where I would be staying and put my suitcase in my room. I was so anxious! I couldn't move fast enough! I pumped, and I walked back to the hospital to be with Michael James.

As soon as I saw him, I felt a huge relief. I wanted to run over, pick him up, and hold him forever! I could not do that. I could only 'look at' him.

He slept most of the time, but I was right next to him. I could reach in and touch him, or lift the clear plastic cover of his isolette and put my cheek on his, or kiss him, but I could not move him or hold him. "His bones are still really soft, so if he is moved incorrectly his bones could develop wrong", the nurse told me. His whole body is extremely delicate!

He was poked in the foot with a needle at least four times a day to keep track of his oxygen level, among many other things. His lungs were not fully formed and there were many things that needed to continuously be examined and recorded. He had to have breathing treatments every two hours. This helped his lungs to develop correctly.

I put the little white teddy bear that my sister had given him, seven inches in length, next to him to show his length, and snapped a picture. The teddy bear looked just the same size as him. He was so tiny, but the little bear looked big next to Michael. I decided that I would use the teddy bear in pictures every other day or so, to show his growth. At about ten o'clock I caught the shuttle back to the 'House' where I'd be staying.

The 'house', was a nonprofit organization that was supported by donations. It made it possible for families who had children, who were in the hospital, to stay close to them. It made it possible for me to stay close to Michael. I had a nice clean room, with a clean bed. I had a phone. I had plenty of food to eat, and a comfortable place to eat, sleep,and shower. I could come and go as

I needed to. There was even a shuttle bus to take me to and from the hospital if I wanted it. There were a few other people who were 'staying there like I was'. We could help each other, even if it was just talking. 'It was a wonderful place. I felt so fortunate to be there. If it wasn't for this 'House', then I wouldn't have been able to stay near Michael.

I was able to eat an apple before I went to my room. I pumped, then I cried myself to sleep as I prayed for wisdom and strength.

I woke up early in the morning and immediately called the hospital to check on Michael. I pumped, and showered. My mind was racing as I moved to get myself ready for the day.

I thought to myself, "If he was still inside of me, he would hear me singing to him, counting to him, saying the alphabet, shapes, and colors to him. He would hear me reading book after book to him. He should be 'inside of me' for three and a half more months. I can't cheat him out of that time!"

As I walked back to the hospital, with my backpack and big breast pump that looked like a large briefcase, I stopped to the store. I bought a disposable camera to keep next to Michael's isolette, index cards, a pen, a pencil, and some markers. I continued to the hospital.

I said good morning to Michael, and gave him a kiss. I just held my cheek on his for a few moments. That was the closest thing to a hug that I could give him. I sat down next to Michael and I started to draw a capital letter of the alphabet on each card. I wrote the lower case letters in each corner. I wrote cards with numbers on them. I wrote squares on cards and colored them different colors and printed the name of the color across the top I also drew different shapes, one per card, and I printed its name above the shape. I very softly spoke out loud, saying everything that I was doing.

I thought to myself, "If he was still inside of me, he would hear me talking all of the time. I wasn't able to 'touch him' while he was in there, but I could 'touch his mind' as I talked. I can't cheat him out of that."

"I can at least touch him now, and I still need to 'touch his mind'." My plan was to, for hours every day, repeatedly go through these cards with Michael, and softly say, "square, s, q, u, a, r, e, square", or. " red, r, e, d, red", or "A, A says 'a' and 'a' ". I said these things in English, Spanish and sign language. I would very softly sing or read to Michael.

'these are part of the alphabet, shapes, numbers, and colors that I made and used as I sat next to Michael'

I took pictures of Michael, of all of the machines that he was on, of all of the needles that were poked into his tiny body, and of all of the hoses that were attached to him. I left the camera right on his bed stand so it was there when needed in the weeks to come.

The next morning as I was showering, I began to remember something from the day before. The nurse had said to me, "the first colors a baby sees are red, black, and white". I put on my cloths for the day, pumped, and started to walk to the hospital, with my 'briefcase' and backpack. I stopped back to the same store and was able to get tape, a pair of scissors, a few sheets of white, black, and red poster board. I also bought a sheet of red and white checkered poster board. As I walked, I was making many designs in my head using the tools and items that I had just purchased.

As I sat next to Michael, I cut and made many different designs out of these colors. I taped up inside of his isolette two or three of these designs to stimulate Michael.

'one of the many tricolored designs that I made and decorated his isolette with'

Throughout the day, as I repeated the flashcards to him, I would also take down the designs and put up new ones. As I was changing these designs, I started to sing songs to him, then I would read a book to him. I repeated this process endlessly until I left at 10:00 that night. I took another picture of the little teddy bear next to him, and caught the shuttle back to the 'House'. I ate an apple, pumped and cried myself to sleep again.

For the next eleven weeks I did not miss a day, being with Michael from eight or nine o'clock in the morning until nine or ten o'clock at night.

As I sat there next to Michael each day, I focussed on Michael but I could still see and hear everything else that went on around us.

I saw and heard how loving, kind, and motherly the nurses were with the babies. There were babies who were born in such bad shape, and these nurses were so good with them, some of them were only there for a short time. The nurses proved to be so 'strong', dealing with this day after day. The nurses all were there because they 'chose' to be there. That told me alot about them as individuals. I felt very fortunate that my son was being cared for by these wonderful people.

I remarked about this to one of the nurses one day while she was caring for Michael. She thanked me, and replied, "people have no idea what goes on up here."

I said, "You're right! I've never read about this anywhere! I've never seen any shows or movies about this."

I have never forgot that ' little conversation' that we had.

Everyday I used the index cards with him, I sang to him, I read to him, I rotated the designs, and I pumped. I continued to take pictures of him. Any procedures that the doctors or nurses did, I was right there next to Michael. Sometimes I was able to share in and help with it.

At about eight weeks old Michael was given one drop of breastmilk through a tube, to stimulate his stomach. (a gut stim). The next day or so it was increased to two drops, then three. It wasn't too long before he was able to take in one or two ounces at once, but still through a tube. I was still pumping six times throughout the day and night, enough milk for a full grown baby, and storing it in little bottles in the freezer in the NICU.

One test that was very hard to watch, was an eye test that the doctors needed to perform.

The nurse would fold a baby blanket in half, spread it flat on the table, and lay Micheal on it so the blanket went across underneath his arms and shoulders. The blanket would be wrapped individually right around his arms, and then his arms were wrapped around his chest and rib area. The ends of the blanket were wrapped and folded together so he could not loosen it. He was then laid in place under the lamp. The nurse would hold Micheal in place while the doctor put a clip into Michael's eye to hold his eyelids open so that he could carry out the examination.

As Michael was held in place on the table, the bright light shined into his eye, and the doctor examined the inside of his eyeball, Michael fought and screamed with all of his strength. He tried so hard to break free. Every few seconds the nurse put drops into his eyes to keep them moist. Then the whole process was repeated in the opposite eye.

The doctor told me that Michael had developed, 'premature retinopathy'. This is an eye disease that can develop in premature babies. It causes abnormal blood vessels to grow in the retina, and can lead to blindness. This examination was repeated every two weeks.

As I sat next to Michael one day, I was approached by the first nurse that had talked to me the day that Michael was born. She told me that there were too many bottles of mine in the freezer, almost two hundred bottles. More were added each day. I told her, "I'm not at home, I can't move them or take them home. I don't want to just throw them away, can I donate them? I see so many babies here that are all alone, no one comes for them!"

She was very happy and she assured me, "there were many babies that would benefit from this, they really need this! It's better than liquid gold for these babies!"

When he was nine weeks old, I arrived at the hospital one morning, and the nurse was working next to Michael. As she wore a big smile she said to me, " I am going to clean him up, and then I want to put clean bedding on for him. Would you please hold onto your son for me while I do this?"

My heart started to race and pound out of my chest! I was so excited to be able to hold my son for the very first time, ever! For the nine weeks since he had been born, I could put my hands in and touch him, but he had to stay inside of his isolette. "Of course I will hold him! I am going to hold my son!" I replied. I felt my insides shaking with excitement!

She wrapped him in several blankets and put him into my arms. She said" his internal thermometer is not working yet so all of his body heat is escaping. You need to cuddle him closely so your body heat keeps him warm."

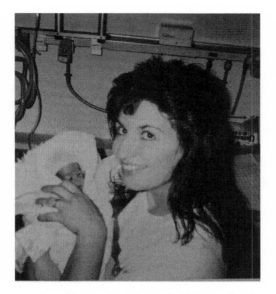

*'I finally was able to hold Michael
when he was nine weeks old!'*

I was so excited to finally be able to hold him close, to cuddle him, to look right into his eyes! After just a few short minutes she took him from my arms and lay him into his nice clean isolette. I felt like I had just had renewed strength and determination pumped into my veins! I felt like I could face and overcome anything that I needed to!

One day, when he was nine and a half weeks of age, I approached his isolate, I saw it was empty! I couldn't help but to picture the worst as my heart started pounding really hard in my chest! I had seen so many babies come up into the NICU, only to disappear. I knew what had happened to them. When I saw their empty isolette, I would swallow hard, and tell myself, "I can't let this happen to Michael! I can't lose Michael!"

One of the nurses saw me in a panic and she very quickly approached me. "Your son is fine" she assured me. "Michael was moved across the hall to the 'Step Down Unit'," which was still part of the NICU, but these babies had progressed past a certain point. We took only a few steps and she was able to point to him, " your son is right there, he's alright". I wiped the tears away and headed toward my son.

As I approached him I noticed that the doctor had taken away his nasal cannula, and instead he wore a piece, a big tube, that had skinny long tubes which were inserted into his nostrils, and it was taped to his face. This was called a CPAP. The other side of this piece was hooked to the side of a hose that was a couple of feet long. His head and neck did not have the strength to move any of these things, so his head was immobilized. To me it looked like Michael was held in place by his nose! One of Michael's doctors was standing at the nurse's station, so I approached and asked him, "Why does Michael need to be on that CPAP? It has him held in place by his nose!"

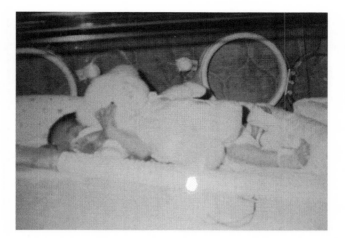

*'the CPAP tube that he needed as he
developed, had him by the nose*

The doctor assured me, "Just like he needed all of
those other important steps that have been taken, he
needs this one as well".

One of the nurses approached me and told me with
a smile, "When we were changing his tubes earlier this
morning, Michael was wide awake. I hope that you don't
mind, but I used your camera to take a picture of him
for you. There was nothing on his face, no tape or tubes,
and his eyes were wide open. He looked right into the
camera. It's going to be a beautiful picture!"

"Oh, please continue to do that, that's why I keep
it next to his isolette." I replied. I was so anxious to see
the photo!

When he was ten weeks and two days old, Michael and I were taken to a little room with a nurse. She said, "Michael is ready to actually start breastfeeding, let's practice a few times so that he will be able to latch on properly". We learned exactly what was needed. I still needed to pump because he was still only taking in a few ounces at a time. I was producing enough milk for a full grown, ten week old baby.

Michael continued to progress, and to grow. I was so happy to be able to hold Michael quite often for short periods of time. He was so beautiful. He had dark eyes and a head full of dark hair. He would look right into my eyes like he was communicating with me. After a few minutes I needed to lay him back into his bed, so as not to let his precious body heat escape, but I would stay right there next to him for hours. I still, each day, for twelve to fourteen hours a day, did all of the flashcards with him, read books to him, sang to him, and rotated the tricolored designs in his isolette. I continued to say things in English, in Spanish, and in sign language to him. I kept telling myself, " I need to stimulate his mind! I need to help him to overcome anything that all of this may cause him!"

Somehow, inside, I felt responsible for this happening. I was taught that by the time a child is two or three years old, their whole personality and characteristics are formed. I had been trying so hard, while I was still pregnant, to develop in him a love for learning, a love for reading.

Now, he was born so early. I have to keep instilling that into him. I can't cheat him out of that! If I didn't help him to develop that, it could affect his whole life, and I would be responsible!

About twelve weeks after Michael was born, any money that I had saved previously was close to running out. I couldn't bear the thought of leaving my precious son to return to work, but I didn't have a choice. I needed to be able to pay the rent so that I had a nice place to bring Michael home to.

I could go into work very early in the morning so that I was able to finish earlier. I planned on driving out to see him each afternoon when I was through work. It was a distance of about fifty miles.

I talked to the head nurse and told her how I needed to change my schedule, but that I would still be there everyday when I was through with work. She promised me that Michael would be taken care of wonderfully.

CHAPTER THREE

On the first day back to work, I received a phone call from the hospital. Immediately my heart started racing! "What happened to my son! What happened to Michael!"

I was told by the nurse that Michael was progressing very well, and was being moved to a hospital in Rome! This was only six miles from the store that I managed! I was so excited! She said, "The ambulance is pulling up to that hospital as we speak!"

"He was so close to home! He was so close to coming home! He was so close to me, only six miles and I can be with Michael! My mind kept repeating this as I tried to work. Somehow, I finished my work, I'm not sure how I did it.

I changed my cloths before I went to the hospital. I had been working in them all day and didn't want to bring germs into the NICU.

I arrived at the new hospital and he was there in the corner area of the NICU. We had our own little 'corner of the room'. I was so happy! He was so much closer to coming home!

There was a wooden rocking chair next to his isolette. I was able to pick him up and rock with him. He was still attached to many tubes and wires so I needed to be extra careful.

I pumped, then went to work very early in the morning. I 'balanced' things from the day before, and did all of the banking. I balanced and recorded the sheets from vendors and much more. I worked really hard to finish all of my work so that I could get out, change my cloths, and go to the hospital to be with Michael. Even though my schedule had changed, I still was there every day with Micheal for as long as I possibly could be.

I pumped in the morning and once or twice during the day, while in my locked office at work. I then stored it in the cooler and brought it with me when I went to the hospital that night.

He was back on the nose cannula for oxygen. I could hold him as much as I wanted to, which was a huge thing to me. I would usually hold him in the rocking chair from the time that I walked in, until the time that I left to go home. He still had tubes and leads attached to him, so I needed to be really careful so nothing came off or dislodged. The three weeks Michael was at that hospital, I noticed a lot of growth in him. The little white teddy bear was getting 'smaller' and 'smaller' each time that I put it next to Michael. He was still very tiny, but he was growing.

One week after I had returned to work, I started to come down with a cold! I was so upset! "This is one of the worst things that could happen right now! I will not be allowed to visit my own son! I could not carry germs into the NICU" I immediately went to my own doctor and started on medication.

It was only two days that I couldn't go to see Michael, but it seemed like an eternity! The nurses were so kind to me every time that I would call on the phone to find out how he was doing. They knew that I was sick so they kept me well informed about Michael.

I regained my health and was able to return to the hospital and to my son. When I walked up to him, and softly started to talk to him, he looked so happy and peaceful laying there. I saw so much growth in him! He finally was able to come out of his isolette for good. He layed in a clear crib, just like a healthy full grown baby lays in! I was so excited to see this!

There were rooms at this hospital where I could take Michael, and all of the supplies that he needed for the night, or all that he needed for a twenty four hour period. The week before he came home, him and I spent time alone in that room as practice for when he came home. They needed to make sure that I would be able to recognize and take care of all that he needed to remain safe. We were alone, but still had emergency call buttons if needed, and all of his monitors were hooked up, so they could still be sure he was alright. It was so nice to be there, alone with my son, but at the same time it was very scary.

While at the hospital with Michael, a nurse handed me a paper, " please read and sign this", she said. It was telling me that on the day before Michael would be released to come home, he would be circumcised. I was excited to be preparing something for when he came home, but at the same time, I was a little bit frustrated.

I asked the nurse, "please ask the doctor if it could possibly be done earlier. After all of the time that he has spent in the hospital, after all that him and I have gone through, do they need to wait until the day before he comes home to do that to him? Do they have to send him home with a sore like that? Why couldn't it be done while he was right here in the hospital?"

The nurse repeated my message to the doctor, and the doctor agreed.

Since I had gone through every other thing with my son, I asked if I would be allowed to be in the room with him. The doctor, at first, told me "no", but finally said, "You are to stand against the wall, with your hands behind your back, and can not move at all, or you will have to leave the room".

The day came for this procedure to take place, I went into the room and stood against the wall, with my hands behind my back. I watched as Michael was put into this little 'cavity' with a cover.' His face was uncovered. I watched as he was circumcised. I felt horrible! He screamed louder than I had ever heard him scream! The doctor and nurses cleaned him up and I was able to sooth him. I felt like the worst mother in the world for allowing this to happen, even though I knew that it needed to be done. Everything healed well, before he came home.

When he was born, he had a head full of dark hair. When he reached his 'actual due date', it all fell out. He had a ring of hair around the sides and back of his head, on top he was bald.

After three and a half months of him being in the hospital, the doctor finally said, " Michael has reached the four pound requirement he is healthy enough, so you can take him home!"

I couldn't believe it! Michael was finally coming home! I was so excited! I was so scared! I was so nervous! I was so anxious, yet relieved! I just started to cry.

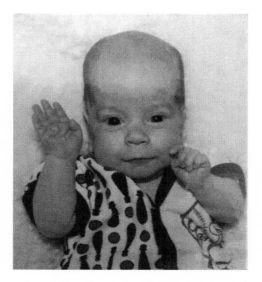

'This should've been his birth picture, but he is exactly fifteen weeks old. It's the day that he came home from the hospital the first time.'

I called the corporate office of where I worked and told them that Michael was coming home and that I needed more time to be out of work. I needed to take care of my son. They gave me no problems.

He came home on a heart monitor. I had our home and the car ready for him to come home, the best that I could. I just needed to grab from my car his bag with clothes and blankets. His carrier was also an infant car seat. I was so excited! Michael James was finally coming home! It was over, or so I thought.

CHAPTER FOUR

Life at home was beautiful, I would turn on the music very softly, and lift up Michael as he was curled up into a little ball. We would face the same direction, and I would put his cheek against mine, and we would gently dance around the room, 'cheek to cheek'. He was so content and happy.

He still slept a lot so I kept his bassinet in the same room that I was in, because I was afraid to leave him alone. He still needed the breathing treatments every two hours, day and night. His feedings were every three or four hours, so my sleep was minimal. I needed to remain very healthy in order for him to be healthy. I still ate mostly vegetables, and drank no alcohol of any kind.

On the second day that we were home, his heart monitor started to beep continuously, telling me that his breathing had stopped. I felt my own heart start to race as I tickled his feet so he would take a deep breath. Then he would continue breathing, until the next time. When this would happen, I was so scared! When he was breathing alright again, I would usually cry in relief. If I didn't keep him very close to me, I may not realize that his breathing had stopped. He was always within three or four feet from me.

It was near the beginning of November when he came home, right at the start of RSV season. Respiratory Syncytial Virus can be very dangerous for toddler and infants. It is DEADLY to premature babies. Their respiratory system is one of the last things to be completely formed before birth. Being three and a half months early, his respiratory system was still extremely delicate and underdeveloped. I could allow no one into the apartment, except for a few certain people, because of the dangers of RSV, and how easily it is transmitted from one person to another. They had to be extremely clean and odor free.

When he had been home for seven days, I looked at him and he was a blueish color. I tickled his feet to make him inhale deeply, then ran downstairs and banged on the landlord's door and ran back up the stairs. The landlord's wife, Karen, was a nurse. She ran up the stairs behind me as I ran and explained, "He's blue! He's breathing really shallow!" I ran right back to Michael and I tickled his feet so he would inhale deeply. Her husband, Robert, was an EMT so he quickly called the ambulance.

She bounced him while tickling his feet every few seconds to keep him inhaling deeply. I quickly threw some things into a backpack, and the ambulance was there in what seemed like seconds. He was put on oxygen for the ride to the hospital. Being on the oxegen brought all of the color back to his face.

He remained in the hospital for three days, I stayed right there with him, except that I drove home to shower and went right back again. It felt different this time because he wasn't admitted into the NICU or even the Maternity Ward. He now was admitted to a single room in the Pediatric Ward. I was not allowed to give his breathing treatments, a nurse needed to give them.

They set up a cot for me to sleep on because I wanted to be in the room with him. This time when he came home, he was still on the heart monitor, but now he was also on oxygen.

There was a large four and a half feet tall oxygen tank in the closet that he was hooked up to, and another one as a backup. We also had a small tank that was portable in case we needed to go somewhere. The hose for at home was very long so I could take him anywhere in the apartment.

When we arrived back home, Michael was either in my arms, or in the bassinet right next to me. I was too scared to take my eyes and hands off of him!

There were a couple of times that I called my landlord's wife to ask if she would come be with Michael so that I could run to the store.

The last few months of pregnancy, usually when you buy everything that you will need for a new born baby, I was at the hospital with him so I hadn't had a chance to purchase too many things. There was no time for a baby shower either. Little by little I was able to purchase the items that he needed.

I had to buy him more clothes. The newborn size clothes that he had were way too big on him. I couldn't find anything small enough for him. I bought many 'one piece pajamas'. They were big on him, but he was warm and comfortable.

I also tried to buy toys for him, to help him develop and learn. Even though he still slept most of the time, I tried so hard to always be conscious of teaching him in any possible way. I continued with all of the 'cards' that I had made. I tried to do things to help him with his coordination and reflexes.

As soon as I had found out that I was pregnant, I had enrolled into two book clubs. I wanted to help him develop a love for books, and a love for reading and learning. Now with so much time at home, we spent many hours reading those books. He loved it when we both would lay on my bed with my head on my pillows and his whole body against the pillow. Our heads were leaning on each other as we read. He would stare right at the book as if he was following along with every word that I read.

Through one of the book clubs, he was slowly getting a set of encyclopedias. We spent many hours reading these together.

The red, black, and white designs that I had made in the hospital, I put on the walls around his crib and by his bassinet. I still used with him the flashcards that I had made, repeating them in Spanish and in sign language. I still sang certain songs to him. I would write little songs to teach him things. The songs that he reacted the most to were the same three songs that I sang to him before he was born, and when he was in the hospital.

After being home for a week the second time, I had to bring him for a check up at his doctor's office. I hooked him up to the portable oxygen, bundled him up, carried the heart monitor, a diaper bag, my purse, Micheal, and rolled the small oxygen tank behind us. We went down the back stairwell, and out to the car. I was able to get it all safely hooked up, and travel to the doctors office, only to unhook it all and carry all of it into the doctor's office.

As I sat in there, children were in there that were sick. I quickly covered his face back up and stood up. As I was rapidly walking out I hollered to the nurse and she followed me. I quickly explained how delicate he was, and said, 'RSV' She immediately went back inside and opened up a side door for us to enter in through that went directly into an examination room. He was examined, and then we exited the same way. That's how we went in and out everytime after that. This way we never went in near other patients that were sick or coughing, so he was sheltered from their germs.

Arrangements had been made by the doctor for a physical / occupational therapist to start coming weekly to help me to help Michael. He was delayed in several areas. She assured me, "as he gets older, he will get closer to where he should be. On the growth charts he is way behind for his age, and on things he should be doing for his birth age, he is behind. His birth is three and a half months early, so inside of his body and his brain, he is still at his gestational age. His gestational age needs to catch up to his actual age. This will take several years."

I added into our exercise routine physical / occupational therapy exercises, which we would do many times each day.

I could see him progressing and growing. His heart machine would start beeping two or three times a week, to tell me that he had stopped breathing. This would start my heart pounding every time, as I tickled his feet to make him inhale deeply.

After being home for six months, the doctor told me, " the readout from the heart monitor shows that his oxygen levels have remained elevated like they should be. His lungs are in much better shape now. We will decrease the level of his oxygen intake." We will try this for one month.

One month later we returned and the doctor looked at his readings again and told me, "We can take him off of the oxygen, but you should still keep it in the closet for a while, in case he needs it back on quickly." I was overjoyed, and scared at the same time. I kept him in the bassinet right next to me. The heart monitor started beeping again but I tickled his feet like I usually did and his breathing continued. The oxygen level in his blood remained elevated like it should be.

At the beginning of April, my leave of absence from work was running out so I needed to return to work again.

A friend of my landlords, who lived just a couple of houses away was prepared to babysit Michael for me. I made sure that she knew how to give his breathing treatments every two hours. I made sure that she knew exactly what to do if the heart monitor started to beep. I also made sure that she understood that he could not be around any odors of any kind. His lungs were too delicate at this point. She started to come to my house to watch Michael.

I returned to work with great difficulty. I was so worried about Michael. I could see his progress, he no longer needed the oxygen that he had been on for so long. He was still on the heart monitor, still had breathing treatments every two hours, and he still had Wolfe Parkinson White.

In the middle of June, Michael came off of the heart monitor also. He had gotten past these obstacles, just like he had gotten past everything else. He still had asthma, and received breathing treatments every two hours, around the clock. He still had Wolfe Parkinson White, and whenever he had an episode, his heart rate doubled for a period of time. It would make him lethargic, or tired, for some time. It took so much of the energy that his little body had.

When Michael was a year old he had an appointment with his cardiologist in Syracuse, regarding the WPW. Many tests were performed. The doctor had an Electrocardiogram and a heart sonogram done. He then said to me, "He definitely is still showing the Wolfe Parkinson White pattern. In time it may correct itself. If it does not, by the time that he turns eighteen years old, I will have to go into his heart and correct it."

When he told me this, there was a very sick feeling in my stomach. Now there was a possibility that my son would have to have heart surgery!

He also went to his eye doctor in Syracuse, to get his premature retinopathy examined. He was held down onto the table the same way as he was while still in the hospital. Now he screamed much louder, and he fought much harder than a year earlier in the hospital. His eyes were progressing well. I also took him to the dentist. There were no problems.

I began thinking about moving to Syracuse area. All of Michael's doctors were out there. If there was any kind of emergency with Michael, he should be near his doctors.

I started to put in job applications around the Syracuse area. I was offered a position as manager of a small store in the city of Syracuse, which I accepted. I searched and found a three bedroom home to rent in a village East of the city, and a daycare for Michael, By the beginning of November, Michael and I moved out to a few miles east of Syracuse.

CHAPTER FIVE

Michael was fifteen and a half months at this point. I loved my new job. I loved our new home. I loved our new life, but I hated the fact that I dropped him off at the daycare by 6:15 am, and didn't pick him up until after 4:30 PM. I felt like someone else was teaching and raising my son, even though every evening and weekend I worked very hard at teaching him. I was also afraid that someone would innocently go around him wearing perfume of some sort, or some other strong odor. They didn't really appreciate how bad that would be for him.

When I picked him up, as soon as we were in the car, I would start trying to teach him. We repeated the alphabet, numbers, colors, shapes, or we would sing songs. Before bedtime we usually curled up together reading books. He still belonged to the two book clubs so he had many books, and we had read all of them, several times. I still also liked to read to him out of one of his encyclopedias.

He received another breathing treatment before he went to sleep. He was in bed by 7:00, I was in bed by 8:30. I set my alarm for 12:30 to give him another breathing treatment.

I often brought work home with me that I needed to get completed at night. Occasionally I would receive a phone call from the alarm company. I had to get Michael up and go back to the store after it closed at midnight because the alarm hadn't been set correctly. I returned back home, twelve miles, gave Michael a breathing treatment, and went to sleep. Only to wake up at three thirty and give Michael a breathing treatment before I got ready for work again. I needed to be there by 6:30 am. I knew it was the best that I could do at this point, but I wanted to be with my son. I wanted to be the one to teach him things, not 'whoever was there working that day'. I kept telling myself, " I need a different job!", but I needed the pay from this one to survive.

The second Sunday in May, the employees who were supposed to work in the store called in. I could get no one to cover for them. I had to go in and work from open to close. This was extremely difficult for me. Not because the work was hard, but emotionally I was a wreck. I was in no mood to work, especially for so many hours. Most people celebrated Mother's Day on that day. Customers came in, talking about their mothers! My mother died on Mothers Day ten years earlier. I had a hard time working that day. I decided right then that I would look for a different job.

CHAPTER SIX

One of the places that I put an application in at was the 'Village Office', in the village that Michael and I lived in. On the application I wrote that I needed to give my present employer two weeks notice. I was soon called and told, "If you are still interested in this position, please turn in your two week notice at your present employment".

I called the corporate office to the store and gave my notice verbally, and then I put it in writing for them. I was excited and nervous! "Had I made the right choice? My new job was so close to home. I needed to find someone very trustworthy to take care of Michael. I started to train my replacement, and the two weeks flew by.

I was able to find a wonderful woman named Cathy. She only lived a couple of minutes from Michael and I. Michael seemed very happy and comfortable with her.

About a month or so after I started that job, I realized that I didn't really care for it. It wasn't a bad job, I just didn't like sitting at a desk all day. Each day I liked it less and less. I continued with it because I had 'responsibilities '.

One day, as I was driving a mile and a half from our home. I drove past the school bus garage for the district in which we lived. I thought about it for a few minutes, then I turned around and went back. I went inside and filled out an application for driving a school bus for the district. It was perfect! It was close to our home, and as soon as he started school we would have the same schedule. I would be home with him every evening and every weekend, and I wouldn't have to bring any of my work home with me. If he had a snow day, so did I! Yes, it was perfect!

I soon received a phone call to come in for an interview. I would start out as a sub driver. The pay was good, and I would have plenty of hours. As time went on I would become a contracted driver, at which time I would get a pay increase, and all of the benefits would start. First, I needed to pass my permit test for driving a school bus.

I 'studied the book' and then went for my 'school bus permit'. I passed the test and received a driving permit to drive a school bus. Then I needed to complete forty hours of training.

The training wasn't completed all at once. It was in increments of two or three hours at a time, a couple of days a week. Before I knew it, the training was completed, and I went for my road test, which I passed.

When school started in the fall, Michael was in pre-k. Each day I was out of bed at three thirty. I worked out and showered. I woke Michael up at four forty five and helped him to get ready. We ate breakfast together, then we sat down on the couch together. We talked and read books for twenty or thirty minutes each morning. I had his heart and mind before anyone else did, and his mind was still clear. If I waited until after we returned home in the evening, we both would have our minds full of what went on during the day. Early morning was one of my favorite times of the day.

I no longer needed to give him breathing treatments every four hours. The doctor had changed them to PRN, or 'as needed'. We would finish talking or reading, and then get ready to leave for the day.

In the winter we needed to go out to start the car, scrape the windows, and brush off the snow. I couldn't leave him alone, so I bundled him up and strapped him into his seat in the back. I wrapped a big blanket around him while I worked outside of the car. It soon warmed up and I brought him to Cathy's house. She soon put him onto the school bus for his morning in pre-k.

I would pick him up from school at eleven thirty, or if I had to drive a bus, his bus would drop him off at Cathy's house. I would pick him up from Cathy's house when I finished, and then bring him back there while I drove for the afternoon.

Cathy had three or four cats, which Michael loved. She did all kinds of crafts and made all kinds of neat things. I felt very comfortable with him there. She also had a son who was a few years older than Michael. His name was Vince.

When we returned home for the evening, we would talk about his day. We would fix dinner together, then eat together, and then clean up together. I was very conscious of making sure that everything that Michael ate or drank was very healthy. He had come so far, but still had a long way to go. I made sure that he didn't eat or drink things that had a lot of additives or chemicals in them.

I would try to teach him so many things. Another favorite part of the day was before bedtime. We would lay on my bed leaning back on the pillows and I would read to him, or he would read to me.

On the weekends Michael and I would do many different things. If we stayed at home, we played games, read books, or played with his toys. He loved it when we built things. We built using large blocks, small blocks, big legos, smaller legos, or tiny legos, magnetic building sets,and much more. He had two sets of little logs. We built so many things using these. Many times we built horse stables with a horse track in the middle. We made so many different horse jumps. In our imaginations, we had many beautiful horses, and had won many races.

Occasionally I needed to stop at the bus garage to pick up my check, or talk to my boss. I needed to bring Michael in with me. He was so tiny, when he stood on his tippy toes, he still couldn't see over the table, and it wasn't a 'high table'!

I had taught Michael, 'not to talk to strangers'. The other drivers loved him, but whenever they tried to talk to him,he would turn away and say, "I don't talk to strangers!". It made me feel proud when I saw him react in this way, because I saw that what I had taught him, he remembered and applied in his life. At the same time, I realized that I needed to make a few adjustments in this area.

I tried to imagine how he felt when he had to ride the school bus for the first time, or how he felt in school. I had taught him 'not to talk to strangers'. Everyone on the bus or in school was a stranger to him, he must've thought that I handed him to a stranger and turned and walked away. He must have been terrified!

I started to introduce him to the different drivers. and they would talk to him a little bit each time that he was in there with me. Once I had introduced them, he became friends with many of the drivers, so it was no longer an issue.

On one weekend one of the drivers came and took Michael for a ride in her 'dune buggy'. He looked so tiny sitting there safely strapped into place. He had so much fun doing that!

The driver's dune buggy that Michael liked so much'

Michael loved to build things, out of anything! I kept paper towel tubes, toilet paper tubes, and boxes of all different sizes. We used these to build with. We designed and made a movie camera, and a robot that was taller than Michael.

We made a race car that he could lift up the top and crawl into so he could actually 'drive it'. We attached four paper plates and drew on them so that they looked like four tires. I picked up for him a black and white racing uniform he could wear when he 'drove his car'.

We took a big box, drew on its side a big square, cut out the top and two sides of the square, and folded it inside. He got his stool from his bedroom and put it inside of the box. He sat on the stool inside of the box, with the 'folded in' part of the box in front of him as a desktop. He wanted to be a 'news man on TV'.

We took a piece of paper and I wrote, "sports" (football and basketball), "weather" (rainy, windy, sunny), "traffic" (accident at the corner, go another way). He told me about sports, the weather, and the traffic accident. I thought that this could help him in public speaking and working from an outline. We had a lot of fun with this, in so many different ways. He was, 'on tv', quite often.

We used cardboard to make a big race track for his cars. We drew the track, some trees, rocks, houses, and much more. He spent a lot of time playing with this, and we needed to remake it several times, each time a different way.

Whenever we were reading, or talking, I would use many illustrations to help him to understand. Sometimes just telling him something wasn't enough, but once I had used an illustration, or a word picture, he would understand. Sometimes we 'played things out', like a puppet show, to help him understand.

A woman that I knew named Jill, had a couple of horses that she used to teach horseback riding. She wanted to teach Michael how to ride because she wanted to enter him in the class for his age group in the horse shows. Once a week we traveled twenty miles north to her farm. At four years old, she was helping him to ride her horse in the horse show.

'Michael's horse show at four years old'

I was raising Michael to be a 'little gentleman'. I taught him to always share with others, to hold the door for others, and to be polite.

One day when I picked Michael up from pre-k, his teacher told me, "Michael does not know his alphabet." I was shocked! We had repeated them just about everyday of his life! I knew that he knew them! He was able to read some of his books to me!

When I picked him up from school the next day, I brought with me the alphabet cards that we used at home. The cards that I had made when he was born. They had been laminated so they kept really well.

I shuffled them so they were not in order, and we went through them. He named them all, capital and lowercase. The teacher and I were both puzzled.

I picked up the ones that were used at school and held one up, and asked, "What's this letter?" He just stared at it. I went to the same letter in our cards and he knew it immediately.

The cards that I made and the books that we read, use basically Roman letters. The school was using D'Nealian letters, which are rounded and have little tails. They weren't 'exactly' what he was used to seeing, so he didn't accept them as 'those letters'.

This was one of the first signs that I recognized that there may be a problem. I didn't focus on it, but I never forgot it. I started using that kind of lettering for him, so he would get used to it. I started to 'see' a few other things that Michael was doing that were 'different'.

He would need to 'touch things, three and four times in a row, in a pattern. As we were walking along, he would need to go back to step in or on something in particular, like a spot on the sidewalk, or a little rock on the lawn. He had great difficulty riding his bicycle. He would have to repeat something three or four times, for instance, touching a door handle. He was very impulsive.

When I would try to help him to avoid doing these things, he became very stubborn, he 'needed' to do these things. He focused on these until they were completed, then he could easily walk away from them. I realized there was something that was making him do these things, but I had no idea what it was.

Each year he went to the eye doctor. Things were progressing well,

I took him to the dentist and was told that there may be problems with his teeth.

When he went to the cardiologist, he still had the signs for WPW. His heart had not corrected itself.

I wanted him to start learning at an early age responsibility and accountability for his actions. I taught him over and over that, "for every action that you take, there is a 'consequence'. It will make something good happen, or make something bad happen. We need to control each thing that we do, each move that we make, and each thing that we say. Before we do or say something, we need to decide what kind of 'consequence' it will bring." If it's bad, we may want to make adjustments so that it will be good.

I was able to find in a store a magnetic job chart. It was a weekly calendar, with many different job titles on magnets so you could change them. I always made sure that his jobs were age appropriate.

We started with things like, 'put your toys away', or 'brush your teeth'. Each day that he did them he received a 'little magnet'. If he had a 'little magnet' all seven days he received a big magnet at the end of the week. For every big magnet that he had, I gave him a quarter.

He tried hard to do everything every day so that he received a handful of quarters at the weeks end. This was a 'good consequence'. He knew that if he only had 'six little magnets' for one of his 'jobs',he wouldn't get a big magnet. He would be missing a quarter. This being a 'bad consequence'. As he grew, his jobs changed. He didn't like to spend his quarters. They usually went into his piggy bank. When that was full, the quarters were rolled and deposited into a savings account for him.

Whenever he would ask, "mommy, can I have 'this new toy', or 'that new toy', I would tell him, "you come up with half of the money and I will come up with the other half." I always paid for the whole thing, but I would give him an extra job or two and he would work hard so he could earn the extra money, so he could 'get more quarters'.

The smile on his face when I put the extra quarters in his hands, and the pride that he felt when he put his half of the cost into my hand was priceless! I always, when he wasn't around, put his quarters right back into his piggy bank. I would buy his 'toy' for him. In his eyes, he worked to pay for half. At an early age, he learned the value of working hard for things that you want in life. He also learned the importance of saving his money instead of just 'running to the store' to spend it on 'anything'.

CHAPTER SEVEN

We decided to go visit my family, that lived sixty miles away. Usually when we went there, we spent the night at Diane's house, my oldest sister. My dad also lived with her. My younger sister, Juliana, also lived in that town, so we would have a nice time each time that we visited there. We would make that 'little trip' about every seven or eight weeks.

I wanted to have some of Michael's friends over for him. We decided that we would make a little carnival. We took some of his toys and made games out of them. I went and found as much cardboard as I could find. Michael and I made a bowling alley for his bowling ball and pins, an alley for the golf ball to roll into the mouth of the crocodile, a background for his velcro darts, a background for his beanbags, along with many other 'adjustments'. We made more beanbags for them to throw through the hanging tire. We made a cardboard bottom for a beanbag three-in-a-row game. We had a total of fifteen games for our carnival.

We cut up paper and made red tickets that they could use to play the games. Each child started out with twenty red tickets, and were given more if they ran out. They were given blue tickets when they won at the games. They used these blue tickets to 'buy' the prizes from the prize box. We had gone to a party supply store and bought prizes for the 'big prize box'.

A few of the bus drivers came and helped me to 'run the carnival'. They each controlled two or three of the games, making sure that all of the kids had fun and were safe.

Jill, the horse trainer, brought her horse from twenty miles away and gave all of the kids rides, for 'two red tickets'.

We had made trays of sandwiches cut in quarters, fruit trays, a big pretzel and cheese tray, and drinks, with cake, cookies and ice cream for dessert. Everything turned out great! We had so much fun preparing for and running the carnival. All of the kids, and their mothers, had a wonderful afternoon!

We cleaned it all up, moving some of our 'games' into the garage so we could still have fun with them.

Michael and I were both very happy and very tired. We both fell asleep early and slept well that night.

Soon after that day as, I sat down and took another look at how my time was managed. I saw where some changes needed to take place. The time that I was spending taking care of the house when things went wrong or yard work, and many other things, I felt that Michael needed this time. I knew that we were going to make it! I had a good paying job, with benefits, and the perfect schedule for Michael. This is where Michael's school was. We were close to all of his doctors.

We moved out of the three bedroom house. To a two bedroom apartment. Here, when something went wrong, I just made a phone call and it would be taken care of, by someone else, not me. Someone else mowed the lawn and cared for it. Someone else shoveled and plowed. We are one mile from where I work. I can walk to work. We are about six blocks from his school, and just two blocks from Cathy's house, This move was definitely a good move for us.

CHAPTER EIGHT

I had seen throughout his life that he does not like change, so it was a definite challenge. I very quickly arranged his bedroom much in the same way as it was in the house. Throughout our apartment I tried to keep groupings of nick nacks and pictures much the same as before. This 'softened the change', for him.

He needed to get his check ups at his eye doctor, dentist, and his cardiologist. All three doctors gave good reports. He still definitely had Wolfe-Parkinson-White, the 'pattern' was still very much active.

Our lives followed pretty much the same daily routine. I was up at three thirty, I worked out and showered. I woke Michael up at four forty five. We ate breakfast together, then we sat together on the couch and read books or talked, sometimes both. Then we got ready to leave for the day. I dropped him off with Cathy and went to drive the school bus. The school bus picked him up, and dropped him off at Cathy's house.

I usually worked at another job in between morning and afternoon runs, then I drove for the afternoon. I went and picked him up from Cathy's house. We returned home and ate dinner. I helped him with homework, played a game or two, got his bath done, we read a few books, and he was in bed by seven thirty, and I was in bed by eight thirty.

On Friday night, when I picked him up from Cathy's, before we were even in the car, I would say to him, "I want sausage and mushrooms, what do you want on our pizza? What movie would you like to watch tonight?"

Friday's were usually our 'date night'. We would order a pizza and watch a movie together. I had joined a movie club several years ago, so I was able to choose and buy movies that were appropriate for him. Our movies never had any bad language or violence in them.

We still kept pretty much the same sleep schedule though. The latest we stayed up was nine o'clock on the weekends. We both had been up since early morning, so we were both tired early.

On the weekend we would do all kinds of things together. We played inside games, or outside games. We went for walks, or went to a local 'game room' for children. We packed lunches in our backpacks and would go hiking for the day. We went to Rochester for the day, or many times, overnight. In Rochester we would go to the zoo, museums or the amusement park.

We always carried outside games and a charcoal grill in the trunk of the car. Every year I bought a pass for the state parks. Sometimes we would pack backpacks and go on a road trip for the day. Many times we stopped in the state parks to grill hot dogs or burgers for lunch. We would take some games out of the trunk, or hike through the park. Sometimes these 'hikes' turned into 'adventures', in the jungle, or we were mountain climbers. We 'traveled all over the world'!

While rock jumping in a creek, we became great fishermen on the 'Yukon', or 'Danube' rivers. Hiking up big hills, we were in the 'Alps' or climbing the 'Rockies'. When we hiked on trails wearing our backpacks, we were in the 'Amazon Rainforest ', or the 'Gondwana Rainforest'! When we walked along the dirt trail by the canal, we were on a 'safari in Africa'. When we were in the dirt and rocks on the edge of the lake, we were 'stranded on a lost island somewhere in the Pacific Ocean'. We truly became, 'world travelers'.

For a while he took piano lessons. I thought that would be good for his finger coordination. For a couple of years he took gymnastics on Saturday. I thought that would be good for his balance and his coordination. I tried so many things and so many different ways to help him in any way that I could.

We used to go out at night with his telescope and look at the stars. We would set the tripod on a small blanket on the hood of the car, or on the ground next to it. One night we saw Jupiter. It was fun when we went in and looked at the poster of the planets on his bedroom door, and then we looked in his encyclopedias. We 'studied Jupiter' and exactly how far away it is.

Other times we would look at the stars in his telescope and talk about how orderly space is, everything following a specific course. Then when we were finished with the telescope, we would go in and look up 'space' in the encyclopedia, or other books that he had. Many times we ended up laying on my big bed looking up at the ceiling talking about what we had seen.

I was able to order through the book club a little light that had two covers for it. One was the northern hemisphere, and the other was the southern hemisphere. It shined the stars onto the bedroom ceiling. He liked finding the different constellations.

One night when we were on our way home, it was dark and we just happened to see the Northern Lights. We parked the car and watched them for a few minutes. The next day we did research in his encyclopedias, on the Northern Lights. We learned a lot.

He also liked it when I took a blade of grass and smeared it onto a glass slide and put another slide on top of it. He looked at it under his microscope. He was amazed that he could see so many things moving around. The more times that we magnified it, the more he was able to see. We used many other things also, other than grass.

I was still seeing him 'touch things, in 'patterns'. He would touch something twice, and then twice again. Every so often, he would change the pattern.

I had been noticing that he was very neat, everything had to be in a specific spot. He could not focus on anything else until things were 'in their place'. I felt bad because I felt responsible. I thought that maybe the move was harder on him than I had thought. It could have been because ever since he was born I 'had to' keep things so clean and neat. Whatever the reason was, I felt responsible.

I wanted to do something for him, so I decided to make a treasure hunt for him. I left a note on the table for him when we came in. It said, "you will find the next clue under, around, on, or in the 'shoes." When he found it, there was a small toy or game with it that started with an 'S'. The clue read, "for the next clue, look under the 'hamper'. There was another little toy near that clue. That toy started with an 'H'. The clues continued that way. If he kept the clues in order it would tell him where to find his 'big treasure'- in the 'shower!' He loved it when I had a treasure hunt for him. We did this quite often.

I tried to figure out ways to help him get use to 'change', because life changes constantly. I would sneak into his bedroom and move one thing, he usually walked into his room and said, "mommy, you've been in here." Every so often, I would change where a piece of furniture was located. Sometimes I changed his jobs for his allowance. I tried to make more and more changes for him. He handled each one better than the last one.

CHAPTER NINE

His teachers in school were very good. Some were more helpful than others were, but he liked every one of them.

When he was in kindergarten, he needed to write down each book title as we read it. The teacher was trying to encourage reading. By the end of the year, we had read so many books together that he won a prize for reading the most books. His prize was a three story car parking garage. It had the elevator for the people, and fuel pumps. He really liked it and played a lot with it.

When in first grade, we made a poster of his favorite book, We worked on it together for a whole weekend. He was so proud of it. After it came home from the classroom, we hung it in his bedroom.

A couple of times during this year, we went to visit the nearby city of Rochester. We attended events at the War Memorial, and we went to the museum of play. We would rent a hotel room, or stay at Betty's house.

We would have a lot of fun going camping. Sometimes we camped up on Lake Ontario, sometimes on Delta Lake, Limekiln Lake, or Nick's Lake. We would ride our bikes all over, go swimming, or go hiking. He especially liked roasting hot dogs or burgers on the fire, or roasting marshmallows. I used to catch mine on fire and he would make me blow it out, because I taught him not to play with fire.

Underneath our living room sofa, we kept a big flattened box. Every once in a while, he would pull it out, crawl inside of it, and roll around in it. Sometimes I would sneak up and stop the box with my leg while he was upside down, he would laugh so hard.

We visited his eye doctor, and the cardiologist. Both gave good reports.

When we visited the dentist, I asked him, "Why aren't Michael's baby teeth falling out?"

We looked at he xrays and the doctor showed me the length of the roots on Michael's baby teeth. His adult teeth were forming 'around his baby teeth'. His baby teeth would need to all be pulled, one or two at a time. This would allow his adult teeth room to come in. A schedule was made so that his baby teeth would be pulled.

Again, a couple of times this year we went to Rochester on weekend trips. We looked forward to these little get aways all year long. We went to events at the War Memorial, or the next trip was the zoo.

We still went on overnight trips to see my family every seven or eight weeks. I tried very hard to make sure that he always had things to do, and things to look forward to.

In third grade, he needed to make a picture board and give an oral report on Brazil. We did a lot of research for information, and we collected several photos for his picture board. We wrote out his report, and he practiced giving it so many times. He received a really good grade for this, he worked hard on it. I remembered him being a newscaster on TV and talking from his outline. I just smiled.

His adult teeth were coming in very crooked because of his baby teeth not falling out. They had been forming and growing around his baby teeth. We were told by the dentist that he needed braces put on his teeth. Arrangements were made and braces were put on.

During the year, we went on our usual trips to Rochester. We attended events at the War Memorial and visited the Museum and Science Center.

In fourth grade, he began receiving help in math. Also, when he had his eye examination, we found that he now needed glasses. It was quite a change for him to get used to.

In fifth grade, the school psychologist talked with me and said, "I feel that Michael has Asperger's syndrome". I went home and did so much research on it. Everything that I found pointed right to him having it. I was in agreement with her.

I talked to his pediatrician about it, and an appointment was set up in Utica with a specialist for this. We went to this appointment, and he was diagnosed as having Asperger's syndrome, to a mild degree, as well as ADHD to a mild degree.

The doctor immediately wanted to start Michael on medications, which I refused. There had to be another way to help Michael to deal with this, other than starting him on medications. I refused to even start with medication.

I read, and read, and read about asperger's syndrome, and ADHD. Many times, in many ways, the kind of food that he eats, or drinks, can have an effect on both of these things. I was already very careful with what he ate and drank. Very seldom did I buy any "junk food'. I learned that Asperger's syndrome is a form of autism. He was nine years old and I finally had the answer. I now knew ---What made him touch things in patterns, ---Why he didn't like change, ---Why he had to follow routines everyday. --- Why he had such a hard time accepting the alphabet as the alphabet, since way back in pre-k. --- Why he learned so much better using illustrations or word pictures. --- Why it took him longer than most to be able to ride his bicycle.---- Why he was such a loner, preferring to be with me or by himself.

I looked at it in a positive way instead of negative. He 'has a one track mind', so, 'he has the ability to focus on something so deeply, able to block everything else out, until his goal is reached'. This is not a bad thing. This would be an asset for him as he went through the rest of school. It would help him so much as he prepared for his future.

His 'stubbornness', I now looked at as 'inner strength, determination, self discipline, and self control'.

I did not want to put him in 'special classes' that would separate him, mark him as 'different'. Even though the school had a wonderful program for children with special needs, I decided against it. I wanted him in regular classes, some with a teacher helper, but still regular classes. I wanted him in the front of the classroom so his focus was on the teacher, not other students. I wanted him in the front half of the schoolbus because he was still so much smaller than the other kids.

I also chose to not tell Michael, at this point, that he had asperger's syndrome. I didn't want him 'to feel' that he was any different than anyone else. After he graduated, he would need to be able to face life as others did, he could not be made to feel 'different' than the other students. He was no different!

He was still so much smaller than other children of the same age. The doctors had said that he would catch up when his body was ready, but as of yet, that had not happened.

In the spring before he turned ten years old, he was invited to be part if a wonderful group of people who were preparing to put on a play at the beginning of the summer. It would be performed in Rochester. We went to rehearsal every Sunday afternoon for about three months.

The time came, we were all nervous, but we had practiced and practiced. The stage was in the middle of the auditorium, Michael and another little boy performed one whole complete scene totally by themselves, in front of four thousand people! It was flawless! I was helping 'around' the stage, but he was 'on' the stage! I was extremely proud of him. He didn't act nervous at all!

When he was in sixth grade, it happened. He started the school year in a size eight, he finished it in a fourteen/sixteen. He constantly needed new cloths because he outgrew them so fast. Now he was the same size as all of the other kids.

CHAPTER TEN

Once in a while he came into the bus garage with me. Some of the drivers who did not see him too often were shocked because they always saw him so little! When his body grew, his voice changed. Now he was almost as tall as me, and his voice was much deeper than it used to be.

Sometimes people would ask me about Michael, "how is he?" I would smile, and say, "he's my best friend".

Many times the person would smile also and say, "that's so nice, that you two are so close."

I thought to myself, I 'need' to be his best friend! I want to be the one he comes to 'for help', or the one that he comes looking for when something great has happened for him. If he doesn't feel close enough to me to come to me for advice, or help, he will get it from someone else, and maybe receive bad advice!" I was so glad we were 'best friends'. I called and had a small dark chocolate cake made for him. The frosting read, "World's # 1 Son"

I picked up the cake before going home. I knocked on the door and I held the cake so that it would be the very first thing that he saw when he opened the door. His eyes got as big around as the cake was! He wanted the whole cake to be his dinner, but of course, he only had a slice.

Each year we continued our trips to Rochester. The zoo, the science museum, a museum of play, are among some of the places that we visited. Sometimes we stayed in a hotel, sometimes we stayed at Betty's house.

For the second time, he was invited to be part of the group that performed a play. This also was in Rochester. Again we rehearsed every Sunday for about three months. The time came and the play was performed, once again, in front of four thousand people. The entire play was performed perfectly. These two experience have been wonderful and beneficial for him. He has learned so much from them!

Each evening when we arrived at home, we would talk about how his day had gone. Most of the time it had gone good, but sometimes, he had a hard day. We talked about what had made it difficult, but, more importantly, we tried to figure out if there was anything that he could have done that would have made it better? Was there something that could have been done differently? Sometimes I would think about it at night, and as we sat on the couch in the morning, we would talk about it.

Sometimes, in the evening, we would think of different, 'what if'... circumstances, and figure out ways to overcome them. We made a kind of 'game' out of it. I felt that this was helping him to learn how to reason on, and resolve many problems that he could face in school, or in life. If and when he was ever faced with something like this, he would be better equipped to handle it.

With the Asperger's syndrome, he needed to follow certain routines, he didn't handle change very well. I was trying so hard to prepare him for changes. I didn't want him to fall apart when things changed. I wanted him to be able to think and reason on it. I wanted him to be able to deal well with changes.

At times we talked about what he wanted to be when he was an adult. He always, for many years, said, "I want to be an architect." He liked designing and building things. I had seen this throughout his whole life. His favorite toys were his building toys, or all of the cardboard that we used to design and build things with.

I had an extra set of keys made so that he could have his own set. I also bought a cell phone for him, in a phone case. This was only for an emergency, or some he and I could keep in contact with each other. I sewed a strap connecting his keys and his phone together, and I attached it to the inside of his backpack. The strap was long enough for him to use his phone or keys without having them become separated from his backpack. This way he never lost his keys or phone. I felt comfortable knowing that he would always be able to open the door to get safely inside, or call me for help.

When he started sixth grade, he no longer went to Cathy's after school. He had proven to me that he could open the door and get in, and lock the door behind himself. When he was inside and the door was locked. He called my phone and left a message that 'he was in'. If he couldn't get in, he was to call the bus garage and they would call me over the two way radio, and I would tell him what to do.

This only happened one time. He called the garage and they called me on the '2 way radio'. I had him walk around and sit on the patio until I arrived at home. He was sitting there when I returned home about an hour later. He was sitting in the shade with his feet up reading a book!

During middle school, we were still best friends, but as his mother, I tried to 'step back a bit'. This was very difficult for me to do. The bond that we had was so strong. When we weren't in school or working, we were together, doing 'something'.

I went out and bought us both metal tennis rackets and some tennis balls. Sometimes we walked to the middle school and played tennis together. Neither of us were too good at it, but we had a lot of fun 'trying'. Sometimes Michael and his friends, Bobby, Adam, or Noah went to play tennis.

Sometimes we would go on bike rides around where we lived, or go play basketball on the courts at the school, and then just swing on the big swings at the school.

Near the end of eighth grade, we attended a program in the high school auditorium. It was about the classes that he would choose during high school. He automatically said that he was going into architecture. We looked at the courses, and we decided that he needed to take construction / carpentry. With the asperger's syndrome, he thought more in pictures, not so much in words. If he learned more about how to build things, from start to finish, and he already had these 'pictures' in his head from building them, he would be better able to 'visualize the process'. This would help him to be able to 'better picture' in his mind what he was designing.

Also, near the beginning of ninth grade, his dentist removed the braces that had been in his teeth for five and a half years. His teeth were beautiful! They were perfectly straight! He had such a handsome smile!

I was so proud if him. Sometimes I sat and thought about him as a baby, he was not supposed to be here! Look at him now! He has come so far! He doesn't 'touch' things anymore, he can handle 'change' much better now, and he doesn't need to follow specific routines anymore. This thought many times brought tears to my eyes. I was so glad that I never had him on medications for Asperger's syndrome or ADHD. I paid really close attention to how different foods affected him. I did so much research so that I had a better idea what I was doing. I was so thankful for him!

The summer between his sophomore and junior years, is when he turned sixteen. He wanted to get his driving permit. I knew that I would need both of his birth certificates, the original one, but also the one when his middle and last names changed to be the same as mine. A month or so before this I started warming him up to the idea of maybe having a sister or brother.

When he saw both birth certificates he learned what his last name was at birth. It really didn't matter to him. That's the day that I told him for sure that he had a half sister. "She is eight years older than you, and her name is Vanessa Smithfield."

I went into my jewelry box and pulled out the two pictures that I had put in their so many years ago. One picture of her when she was eight years old, and the other one of her also eight years old holding Michael as a baby. With those two pictures, I kept her mom's old phone number. I had kept track of her all of these years so that, when the time came, I could help them find each other, if they wanted to.

I called her mom and said, "I told him, please take my phone number and give it to Vanessa. Please have her call me, when and if she would like to talk. Within a half of an hour Vanessa called my phone, in hysterics! She was so excited!

That evening Michael and her talked, on speaker phone, on Michael's phone. Her mom and I talked, also on speaker phone, on my phone! They were in different houses, and we were unable to do a 'three way call'. We talked for over an hour, passing pictures back and forth on our phones.

In one day, he got his driver's permit, gained a sister named Vanessa, a brother in law named Kevin, a niece named Melissa, and a nephew named Peter. He was so happy! He was smiling from ear to ear! After that they talked quite often.

We practiced driving my car, but I felt that he would benefit from taking professional driving lessons. I made some phone calls and set this up for him. Twice a month, on Saturday morning, he would have his driving lesson.

In August, we were at home one afternoon, and it started to look weird outside. I turned on the news and learned about a tornado watch. We ran upstairs and invited our neighbor to come down to our apartment. We lived in the lowest apartment. We also helped the blind woman, who lived next to us, into our apartment with us. She was by herself so we knew she needed help. We all huddled in the hallway outside the bathroom door. We had our phones, waters, a little bit of extra food, and heavy comforters over us. The tornado went through and we were all safe! The streets were a mess, but we were all safe.

About a month later, I called Vanessa's mom and made a suggestion that we get those two together, but I wanted it to be a total surprise for Vanessa. She was eight years old, and her baby brother just disappeared. I felt really bad for that, but I had no control. Her mom and I arranged for us to meet at the 'Farmer's Museum', ninety miles away from where we lived.

Michael didn't know where we were going that morning until we were about halfway there. I finally told him and I explained that Denise, Vanessa's mom, would text me as they arrived. He became 'so excited!' Him and I arrived and went inside.

Suddenly, I received her text, several of them! "we are pulling up!", "we are parking the car!", "we are walking in!", "we are paying the cashier!". I peaked around the corner and I saw them!"

We were hiding around a corner, and as they walked by, I pulled Denise towards me, and Michael stepped in her place. He was now walking right behind Vanessa! He reached up and tapped her on the shoulder. She turned around and yelled, "Oh my God! Oh my God! What are you doing here?" She recognized him from the pictures that we exchanged. She looked at her stepfather and her husband, and as she threw her arms around him, she said, "It's Michael ! It's Michael !"

Her mom and I just stood back I bit, watching them, both of us wearing a big smile on our face. Finally, after so many years, they had been reunited.

We spent most of the day at the farmers museum with Vanessa and her family, part of Michael's new family. She introduced Michael and I to her children as Uncle Michael and Grandma Eileen, and she called me 'Mom'. I was very touched.

After all of these years, she remembers baking cookies together, doing our hair, putting on makeup, holding Michael and sleeping next to his crib. Michael and Vanessa walked around and around talking and laughing.

"Uncle Michael, I want to ride the Merry Go Round with you! I want to sit right next to you! Let's sit on this seat!", (it was a horse carriage), said five year old Peter. Michael's face, as he looked down at his nephew, was a look of pure happiness and pride!

As he carried around one year old Melissa, he held onto her and looked at her as if to say, "this is mine, this is my niece!" His smile didn't leave his face all day long.

We sat down for lunch together, we talked about so many things, and we took a lot of pictures. We took pictures of everyone together, or separate, of him and his brother in-law Kevin, who seemed rather quiet, but very kind. He stayed in the background and watched over their children.

All of us went on a wagon ride together. We went to the cow barn and Michael learned how to milk a cow! Vanessa and Kevin help to run Kevin's parent's farm so they had fun watching Michael try it! Vanessa and Michael tried to catch a swinging apple, with their teeth! They also learned how people used to grind corn by hand.

As the day came to an end, they stood right next to each other and had a really nice picture taken. They looked so much alike! It's was very obvious that they were brother and sister!

They talked to each other quite often on the phone, and about once every seven or eight weeks we went to see them on the farm. Peggy, Vanessa's mother in law, took me to what is now one of my favorite spots on the farm. It's in the back, up in the fields. Way up on top of the hill there is a gazebo. At the gazebo you can see for twenty or thirty miles, looking away from the village. It's in the middle of the pasture so cows could be walking around you, and the pond is close to it. It's the highest point around there.

Peter and Melissa like to take Michael or I by the hand and walk us out to the barn. They like to show us their calves, or tell us about milking the cows.

CHAPTER ELEVEN

As Michael started school again in the Fall, he had matured a lot over the Summer. He was starting his first year in construction / carpentry, and very excited about it. We needed to go and purchase his toolbox, and a list of tools. We also bought a good hardhat and safety goggles.

Each school year, the carpenters built a house, free of labor fees but the homeowner bought all of their supplies for building his house. The first year that he took construction / carpentry, the class built a really nice solar powered, water heated house. Water tubes ran through the floors to heat it as well as cool it.

When his class was building that house, a local TV station did a little segment about them. It was a wonderful experience for him. He saw himself on a real TV, not just one that we had designed and built out of cardboard, like when he was so much younger.

From his experience building that house, he decided that he didn't want to be an architect, he wanted to go into Solar Engineering. He was still designing things, like he's done his whole life. He's always liked doing that. We designed and built so many things out of cardboard when he was little. He loved building with his blocks and magnets too, but that was so many years ago.

By the end of the year the house was finished. It was an absolutely beautiful two story house, with an attached garage. He couldn't wait to show his pictures of it, and the news segment, to Vanessa when we visited her and her family.

Right at the start of his senior year we could order his class ring. We looked and looked. He decided on getting a necklace instead of a ring. He said, "I will be able to wear it longer, and it won't catch on any electrical tools that I'm working with and damage my hands."

When I heard him make that statement, I smiled. He was thinking ahead, thinking of the consequences before he made the decision. I had been teaching him to do that since he was so little. It was so nice to see him applying it. He chose a black onyx stone, with a silver casing for his senior necklace.

It was also time to have his senior pictures taken. One of the retired school bus drivers ran a photography studio, and he agreed to take pictures for Michael. In his studio he took many pictures in different outfits, pictures next to his fancy sports car, and then we went to the nearby state park. There were pictures by the lakes, in the trees, at the golf course, and the hills overlooking the lake. There were over one hundred and twenty pictures on a computer disc for us.

In his senior year of high school, his construction / carpentry class built an addition onto an already existing home. They did a really nice job. Again, he learned a lot. He was still going into solar engineering.

Sometimes I thought of him when he was so tiny, laying so helpless, in the isolette in the hospital. Now he was reaching adulthood, building houses! I felt so proud of him!

We had meetings at the high school preparing for college. He didn't want to stay in a dorm with so many people around. He said, "There is so much that could go on in a dorm. I've got too much going on, too many things that I need to focus on, for me to be sidetracked. I need all of my attention to be on my classes!"

Again, I just smiled. My little boy was thinking in such a mature way. He was thinking of the consequences before he acted, before he made his decision. He had been taught that his whole life. He made me 'So Proud'!

He chose a local college for the first few years. He would be able to stay at home. He was accepted.

Near the end of his senior year, he needed to have his yearly checkup with the cardiologist. Many different tests and exams were performed, then we had to go into the doctor's office to talk. With a huge knot in my stomach, we sat there. So many years earlier this doctor told me, "If the WPW doesn't correct itself by the time that he's eighteen years old, I will need to go in and correct it."

This was it! In the next few minutes I will know if my precious son will need to have heart surgery, or not!

The doctor walked in, and smiled. When I saw that, in my heart, I knew. I also smiled.

He said, "The Wolfe Parkinson White is still present". My heart sank! Then he continued, "I think that we do not need to go in at this point. He is having no problems with it at this time. If in the future it becomes a problem, we will run more tests at that time." He showed me the test results, 'the increase of physical activity, and the reactions of the WPW pattern".

Michael did not need heart surgery! I felt so relieved! I had dreaded this day for so many years! He will continue to get checkups every two years. This is one more thing that he has been able to get past.

When graduation time came, his class was too large for it to be held at the high school. It was held at one of the local colleges. His grandfather, my dad, came, and Cathy. I felt so proud of him! My little one pound twelve ounce son, born fifteen weeks early, who wasn't expected to live, is alive, and has overcome so many things! He's walking across the stage and accepting his diploma!

He's worked so hard to get to this point, usually averaging the high honor roll. In elementary school he received extra help with math. Now he was choosing a career that involves a lot of difficult math! Throughout the years in school, he was in some classes with a teacher helper. As he has gotten older, he has gotten past that, and needed no extra help. We found out that he has Asperger's syndrome and ADHD. With a lot of research and determination, he has learned how to deal successfully with these. Now, no one could even tell that there had been any kind of problem of any sort.

I looked at him with a big smile, as his diploma was put into his hand. I smiled, and cried, at the same time. My 'walking miracle' was graduating, at seventeen years of age! The pride that I felt at that moment was incomparable!

I wanted so much to give him a graduation party, I've saved for, and I have had it all planned out for a long time. He told me over and over again that he didn't want it. He wasn't comfortable with a lot of people around. Instead he wanted me to take whatever money that I would've spent on a party, and put it into his savings account. So, I did. I took him out for a very nice dinner instead of a party.

The very next day we went to my hometown where I grew up. My younger sister, Juliane, still lives there. Her son, Andy, was born three days after Michael was, so he too was graduating.

We attended his graduation and then we went to a small cookout for him. Later that afternoon, they both put on their graduation gowns and took pictures, the two of them together, and then the two of them with my father. My dad, 78 years old, stood in the middle of his two youngest grandsons. All three wore big smiles that day, and so did I.

CHAPTER TWELVE

It was all set in place for him to attend a local college for a couple of years to receive his associate's degree in Engineering. Then he would transfer to another college for his bachelor's degree, and possibly his master's degree.

We still kept the same schedule. I was up at three thirty, and he was up at four forty five.

He would catch the city bus at seven o'clock in the morning, I would drive for the morning, go to my second job and drive a noon run. I then would drive back to the bus garage of my main job and drive my afternoon runs and my late run. Then I would pick him up after I finished work each night. It was a twenty five minute drive one way, so this became one of our times to talk about how the day went, good things or bad things.

Once in a while his friend, Bobby, from high school rode home with us, as he was attending the same college and rode the bus with him each morning. We arrived back home by six fifteen. We would fix dinner, eat dinner, and clean the dishes. I showered, and was in bed by eight thirty. He was in bed by nine o'clock.

His sister was pregnant, soon to give birth to their third child. She gave birth to a healthy little girl, named Sarah. Michael was so proud of the fact that he now has one nephew and two nieces.

We were still very close, still best friends, but he didn't 'need me' the same way that he used to 'need me'. He was now able to do things for himself, he had grown into a very responsible adult. I didn't need to meet with his professors, or make arrangements or appointments for him, he takes care of things. He is still my best friend, and we are together most of the time when we're not working or in school.

Years ago, before Michael was born, I used to write a lot of poetry, and other things. Many of them I had copy written in the Library of Congress in Washington DC. When he came along, I dropped everything else. He became the center of my life. My life revolved around him.

Now that he was old enough, and he 'had his feet under him', 'he had a good foundation', I began to 'write' again.

I was telling one of my bosses about my writing. I read her some of the things that I wrote 'so long ago'. I told her that I'm going to start writing again. She said, "You need to write a poem for your son."

I told her, "yes, I've been thinking about that. I have many ideas rolling through my mind."

I went to pick him up that night from college and had to sit and wait for him to come out. I wanted to write a poem about Michael. I thought and thought...

Michael James, my son, where do I begin,
Right from the start you've brought joy,
As soon as I knew I was expecting,
What I truly wanted was a boy,

I went into labor at twenty three weeks,
In full labor for nine and a half days,
"If born at this time, he won't make it they said", They tried to stop you in so many ways,

You came very early, three and a half
months,
One pound twelve ounces was
Your lungs were not formed, and
The doctors said, "now

I had to stop because Michael came out. I had to
quickly wipe away the tears before he opened the door.
We drove home.

I thought about it throughout the whole evening,
and as I was trying to go to sleep.

The next morning we were up at the usual time. I
got ready and I left for work, and he caught the bus at
seven o'clock, an hour and a half after I left. I finished
for the morning, and instead of going to my other job,
I went home to write.

Every time that I would try to think of the words that
I needed to write down, I would be right back there, going
through it all over again. 'I was looking up at the ceiling
in the hospital as I laid in bed praying that he not be born
yet! I could 'hear' him 'not crying' when he was born. I
could see the nurses passing him to each other in the labor
room. I could 'see' him crying, I would 'see' him calm
down when he heard my voice, or when I quietly sang to

him. I could 'see' him having an eye exam, screaming as his eyelids were clamped open! I saw him wheeled up next to me in the isolette after he was born.

"Oh no! I ran out of time! I'm going to be late returning to work!", I hollered in a panic! I had been lost in thought for three hours !

I returned to work for the afternoon, and I thought all evening and night. I woke up in the morning still thinking about my poem. When I went home after the morning run I needed to write again.

> "He has WPW" the doctor said,
> It's an extra passageway in your heart,
> Your heart rate
> So scary
>
> In the hospital for three
> With so many
> You came home, then went back
> On machines, and with tubes
>
> There were so many times that
> Telling me that your breathing
> I would tickle your,
> You'd be fine for awhile

The breathing treatments
First two years it
It then changed to three,
Your lungs were improving,

I stopped writing to return to work for the afternoon bus runs. After I finished driving, I parked my school bus and punched out, I had a twenty five minute drive to pick up Michael at the college. I thought about the poem all of the way there. It was very hard thinking about it because it brought back so many difficult memories. Other car drivers gave me some funny looks because I kept wiping away tears.

I texted him and told him that I was there. He texted me back, "I'm going to be a little bit late, I'm talking with my professor."

I sat there in my car, waiting and thinking...

There were so many
You conquered them just
Then, at nine years ol
Asperger's

That didn't stop you, you
You gained

You overcame each a
So much better than

And then came your
You took your
You wore a big smile
As

Now you're in your
En
You are working so hard to
In a few years,

You have grow
So determined,
You're polite, so well mannered,

With your

I want you t
Of all that you are,

I sent him a text that he could read as soon as he was finished with his professor. "Michael, will you please proofread this for me, it's pretty important to me."

A few minutes later, he texted me back. He said, "Thank you mom! Thank you so much! I love it! Thank you!

I was reading his reply with a big smile, because I was imagining his face as he read my message. Just then he opened the car door. He was wearing a big smile, just like I pictured him. He smiled all of the way home, repeatedly thanking me.

I felt that this was one of the best things I had ever written. Maybe because there was so much meaning in it for me.

What I wrote to him definitely came right from my heart, it read:

MY DEAR SON

Michael James, my son, where do I begin,
Right from the start you've brought joy,
As soon as I knew I was expecting,
What I truly wanted was a boy,

I went into labor at twenty three weeks.
In full labor for nine and a half days,
"If born at this time, he won't make it", they said,
They tried to stop you in so many ways,

You came very early, three and a half months,
One pound twelve ounces was your weight,
Your lungs were not formed, and you had several tubes,
The doctors said, "now, we just wait",

"He has WPW", the doctor said,
It's an extra passageway in your heart,
Your heart rate was over three hundred at times,
So scary it was, on my part,

In the hospital, for three and a half months,
With so many changes taking place,
You came home, then went back, then came home again,
On machines, and with tubes on your face,

There were so many times that the machines went 'Beep'!
Telling me that your breathing had stopped,
I would tickle your feet, so you'd take a deep breath,
You'd be fine for a while, as 'my heart' stopped,

There were breathing treatments you needed to have,
First two years it as every two hours,
It then changed to three, and then went to four,
Your lungs were improving, 'gaining much power',

There were so many things, one by one, you got past,
You conquered them just like a champ,
Then, at nine years old we were told, "there's more".
Asperger's syndrome they now said that you had,

That didn't stop you, you didn't even slow down,
You gained strength and kept forging ahead,
You overcame each aspect of asperger's,
So much better than doctors had said,

And then came your graduation from high school,
You took your diploma, and walked across the stage,
You wore a big smile, and stood up so tall,
As your life's book turned to the next page,

Now you're in your second year of college,
Engineering is what you have picked,
You are working so hard to accomplish your goal,
In a few years, this too, you'll have licked,

You have grown into such a wonderful person,
So determined, so focused, so strong,
You're polite, so well mannered, truly gentleman like,
With your loving heart, you can not go wrong,

I want you to know the pride that I feel,
Of all that you are, that you've become,
I couldn't be happier, I want the world to know,
That you are, Michael James, my dear son.

When we arrived at home, I made sure that we made a couple of paper copies for us to keep. I added mine to my collection of poetry. I soon had it copywritten in the Library of Congress in Washington DC with my other poetry.

He changed his major from solar engineering to mechanical engineering. For solar engineering he would need to transfer to a college where he needed to stay in a dormitory. He will take mechanical engineering at a local college so he can still stay at home. Here he can have 'better focus on his classes, and not be sidetracked', this being his choice.

Michael and I are still each others best friend, even though he is a young adult. I have continued with my writing, while still driving school bus. Down the road when I retire, I will be able to give a little bit more time and focus to my writing, and other things.

Michael, the one that I was told "would not make it", he will be going on for his bachelor's degree in engineering, possibly his master's degree. Then we shall all see, what he does with his future, because he 'SURVIVED'!!!!

44041147R00066

Made in the USA
Middletown, DE
02 May 2019